50 WACKIEST BIBLE STORIES

stjohn southallgreen
growing together in christ

Presented to:

Oscar Poulson

I will sing to the Lord all my life;
I will sing praise to my God as
long as I live.
Psalm 104 v 33

Summer 2014

50 WACKIEST BIBLE STORIES

Andy Robb

CWR

Published 2013 by CWR, Waverley Abbey House, Waverley Lane, Farnham, Surrey GU9 8EP, UK. Registered Charity No. 294387. Registered Limited Company No. 1990308.

See back of book for list of National Distributors.

Unless otherwise indicated, all Scripture references are from the Good News Bible: Old Testament © American Bible Society 1976, 1992; New Testament © American Bible Society 1966, 1971, 1976, 1992

Concept development, editing, design and production by CWR

Cover image: Andy Robb

Printed in China by 1010

ISBN: 978-1-85345-983-2

Intro

Congratulations!

Buying this book is one of the smartest decisions you'll ever make if you're wanting to get your teeth into the Bible but aren't quite sure where to start. Not only have we hand-picked some of the best bits for you, but we've also chopped them up into nice, easy-to-chomp morsels. How's that for thoughtfulness?

In this tasty book we've served up fifty juicy, bite-sized bits of the Bible to munch on and loads of crazy cartoon pics to make them easy for you to digest.

To keep you on your toes, we've mixed up the Old and New Testament stories. Not sure what the difference is between them? It's simple. New Testament stories kick off from when Jesus showed up on planet Earth. The Old Testament happened before that and goes right back to the beginning of time.

But if you're thinking that this book is all about being spoon-fed stuff from the Bible so that you don't have to lift a finger, think again!

At the end of each Bible bit there's some investigating work for you to do, which means you'll need to get your hands on a Bible if you want to find out how the stories end.

Just in case you've bought this book but you don't know much about the Bible, let me give you some useful facts …

Fact number one:
Although the Bible is one book (and what a whopper it is), it's actually made up of sixty-six mini books.

Fact number two:
The Bible wasn't written by just one person like most books. It has over forty authors.

Fact number three:
The Bible was written over a period of roughly 1,500 years.

Fact number four:
Everything that's in the Bible was God's idea.

Next up, you're gonna need to know how to read the Bible – and I don't mean from left to right and top to bottom.

The first thing to know is that every Bible book has got its own name, such as Joshua, Judges, Job, Jeremiah, Joel, Jonah, John, James or Jude. To make these Bible books easier to read, they're handily divided up into chapters (like normal books)

and then each chapter is broken up into verses (like you get in poems). All clear so far? Good!

So, if you wanted to check out Bible book Genesis, chapter 5 and verses 25 to 27, here's how it's often written down:

Genesis 5:25-27

Check out these verses and you'll discover who the world's oldest man was (ever) and how many birthday cards he would have received if they'd been invented way back then (which they hadn't).

That's about it.

So what are you waiting for? Tuck in!

ow do you get to school each day? Do you walk, do you cycle, do you take a bus or a train, do you have a ride in a car? Well, I thought you'd be fascinated to hear about some amazing stories from the Bible of some out-of-the-ordinary ways of getting around.

First up is a story featuring none other than Jesus. He'd had a busy day teaching the crowds (who hung on His every word) about God, healing the sick and then ending the day miraculously feeding 5,000 people using just five loaves and two fishes that a young lad had given Him. After a full-on day like that Jesus needed to take some time out with God and to recharge His batteries, so He sent His disciples (the bunch of men who went everywhere with Him) on ahead of Him and headed up a nearby mountain for some prayer time.

Meanwhile the disciples had set off in their boat for the other side of Lake Galilee but very soon the wind blew up and they found themselves slap bang in the middle of a rather scary storm. Just when the disciples thought that things

couldn't get any worse, they did. Heading in their direction was what looked like a ghost. Aargh!

But then the penny dropped. It wasn't a spooky spectre after all. It was none other than Jesus. Hang on a minute. How did Jesus get out into the middle of the lake without a boat? He must have walked on the water to get to them. Why didn't they think of doing that? It would have been easier than rowing.

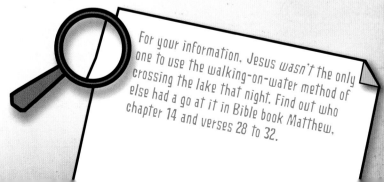

For your information, Jesus wasn't the only one to use the walking-on-water method of crossing the lake that night. Find out who else had a go at it in Bible book Matthew, chapter 14 and verses 28 to 32.

2
TRANSPORT TALES NO.2

Have you ever been on a journey where you've had to change along the way? Perhaps you've had to change trains. Maybe you've gone from a taxi to an aeroplane. And when you were little there's every chance that you'd have been taken from your car and transferred to a child's buggy.

Well, fasten your seatbelts because this next transport tale will beat 'em all. It stars a guy called Jonah who was a prophet of God. Jonah had a bit of a problem on his hands. Actually he had a very *big* problem. The problem was this. God had given Jonah the job of telling the nasty Ninevites that He was giving them one last chance to quit being bad. If they didn't, God would call time on their wicked ways and destroy the lot of 'em.

Jonah was more than happy to go along with the 'destroying the lot of 'em' bit but he wasn't too keen on the 'giving them one last chance' bit. As far as jaded Jonah was concerned the rotten enemies of his nation deserved everything they had coming to them. No way did he want God to let them off the hook. So Jonah took a boat in the opposite direction and hoped that God wouldn't notice he'd scarpered. But God did.

God stirred up a stinking storm and when the sailors on the boat found out that Jonah was to blame they flung him overboard … and the storm subsided. Was that the end of the road (if the sea can have roads) for Jonah? Not yet! This was simply God's way of transferring the runaway prophet to a different means of transport and of getting him back on track. Which is why a ginormous fish swallowed Jonah whole and kept him stowed away for three dark days in its bilious belly.

TRANSPORT TALES NO.3

In the previous story we heard about how Jonah travelled to Nineveh by fish (if you don't believe me you'll have to read the story), but I think this next Bible bit about unusual methods of transport is going to astound you even more, if that's at all possible. Here's what happened.

A Christian called Philip had been busying himself telling people about Jesus. He'd arrived from Jerusalem where a guy called Saul had been giving the followers of Jesus a hard time by having them rounded up and thrown into jail. Many of the Christians made a quick exit and Philip was one of them. He ended up in a place called Samaria where he wowed the crowds by performing loads of miracles in God's power. Loads of people became followers of Jesus because of what Philip said and did.

Just when everything was in full swing, an angel of God showed up and told this power-packed Christian to head south to the desert road out of Jerusalem. Philip did as he was told and very soon found out why God had sent him there. On the road out of the city came a chariot carrying an important royal official from Ethiopia.

Philip must have been pretty fit because the Bible tells us that he ran along beside the chariot and took a sneaky look inside. At that precise moment the chap was reading all about Jesus, but he hadn't a clue what it meant. Philip was invited on board and he explained that it was all about how people can be friends with God, because of Jesus. The Ethiopian official was so convinced by what Philip said that he stopped the chariot and asked Philip to baptise (dunk) him in a pool of water at the roadside (as a sign that he'd also become a Christian). Well, that's the build-up. Now here's the punch line.

TRANSPORT TALES NO.4

The Bible has plenty of stories about heaven including one about a fella called Paul who had a vision of what heaven is like. It was so awesome that Paul found it difficult to put into words. Then there was Jacob who had a dream about the place while he was sleeping, of a ladder stretching up to heaven with angels going up and down it. And not forgetting a chap called Enoch (pronounced Ee-nok) from early on in the Bible. He was actually the great-great-great-great-great grandson of Adam (the world's first man) if you must know. Enoch's claim to fame is that he went straight up to heaven without ever dying. Nice one Enoch!

But the story about heaven that we're going to dive into now is probably one of the most impressive. If you've ever seen someone really important like a president or a royal ruler you'll notice that most times they travel in big limos or ornate carriages flanked by loads of outriders. You only get that travel treatment if you're someone special but that's precisely what happened to Elijah, a prophet of God.

To be honest, being one of God's prophets was not the best paid job and for most, if not all, of the time Elijah travelled around on foot. Elijah was well aware that his time on earth was up and so was his assistant Elisha, but I'll bet that neither of them could have imagined the celebrity travel treatment God would give Elijah to get him to heaven.

TRANSPORT TALES NO.5

Saul was an important religious bod in and around Jerusalem but all that changed when he was travelling to Damascus to stir up things against the Christians. Jesus interrupted his travel plans big time and not only changed Saul's heart so that he became Jesus' biggest fan but He also changed his name (to Paul).

Now it was *Paul* who was having the hard time. Wherever Paul went to tell people about Jesus *he* was met by opposition. The religious leaders were the worst troublemakers. Not only did they think that Paul was a traitor for turning his back on their Jewish religion (or so they thought) but they also thought he was bonkers. Paul was so sold out for Jesus that this didn't bother him a jot but that didn't mean things were easy.

The religious leaders were baying for blood. As far as they were concerned, the sooner Paul was out of the way the better. They'd had enough of him touring the region turning people's hearts to God (and away from them). Paul must have been used to travelling in style when he'd been one of the top religious leaders but now things were rather different.

Being on the road for Jesus was rough and tough. When Paul finally arrived in Damascus he was a changed man and wasted no time in telling the Jewish people there that Jesus was the reason for this transformation. He told them straight out that Jesus was the special person (sent by God) that the Jewish religion had been waiting for throughout their history. They called this special person the Messiah.

To the horror of the religious leaders some of the people began to believe what Paul was saying. Paul had to be stopped and pronto.

Want to find out how this nail-biting story ends and the unusual method of transport Paul used to make his getaway? Head for Bible book Acts, chapter 9 and read verses 23 to 25.

TRANSPORT TALES NO.6

6

ere's a question for you. How would you transport a box that's not much bigger than your average coffee table? I guess you could get a couple of people to carry it or maybe put it in the back of a van. Well, in the Bible story we're about to look at, King David of Israel got himself in a bit of a pickle and it was all to do with how he carried a box a bit like the one we've been talking about.

Okay, so this was a rather special box. In fact it was so special that only Israel's Levite tribe had the thumbs-up from God to carry it. This box was called the ark of the covenant and inside it were mementos of some amazing miracles God had performed. The ark box also represented God being with the Israelites so whenever the ark was around, everything seemed to go well for them.

For twenty years this special box had been stored at the home of a guy called Abinadab but Israel's king figured that it was time to bring it back to their capital city (Jerusalem). With loads of whooping and celebrating the ark box was loaded on to a cart and off they set for the road trip back to Jerusalem.

To be honest the roads in those days were little more than dirt tracks and it should come as no surprise to you that one of the oxen pulling the cart suddenly tripped on the uneven ground. The cart lurched and it looked like the ark was going to plummet to the ground.

One of Abinadab's sons (Uzzah) who'd been part of the procession raced to the rescue and grabbed hold of the ark box to stop it falling. Bad move! This sacred box was not to be touched by any Tom, Dick or Harry (or Uzzah) and God struck him down dead. Gulp! King David wasn't taking any chances and he left the ark at the home of a fella called Obed Edom. The good news is that David soon found out that there was a right way to carry the box and a wrong way.

To find out what that is go to Bible book 1 Chronicles, chapter 15 and verses 11 to 14.

ODD WAYS OF DOING THINGS NO.1

Joshua was a chap you might have heard about. God had given him the job of leading the Israelites into the land of Canaan which was going to be their new home. The only thing getting in the way was the River Jordan, but God soon sorted that by clearing a pathway through the water for them. So far, so good.

Now they were finally in Canaan all that was left was for everyone to find a patch of ground to live on and to settle down. Easy peasy. Er, not quite. There was just the small matter of the people who already lived in the land. They'd have to be got rid of first before anyone started building homes and planting flower beds. As if that wasn't enough, many of the towns and cities were surrounded by whopping great walls to prevent intruders (like the Israelites) from getting in.

The first of these cities was a place called Jericho. Before they'd had a chance to scratch their heads and to ponder how on earth they were going to conquer it God came to the rescue, but with an extremely odd strategy. They weren't to lift a finger for six whole days. No fighting. No attacking. Nothing. All God wanted them to do was to march in a long procession around the city walls, once a day, for six days. And that was it.

I wonder what they felt like strolling round and round the city walls for six whole days in full view of the people of Jericho? If the inhabitants were getting complacent then they had another think coming. Day seven was about to change everything.

ODD WAYS OF
DOING THINGS NO.2

Jesus always seemed to be full of surprises, even for those who knew Him well. One time He needed to feed a crowd of around 5,000 people who'd been following Him on His travels. With just a couple of fish (and a few loaves of bread) Jesus fed the lot of 'em. Amazing!

On another occasion some of Jesus' disciples (the men who followed Him round) were coming into shore after a rubbish night's fishing. Jesus told them to give it another go and to throw their nets out one last time. Reluctantly they did so and were gobsmacked when they pulled in a bumper haul so big it nearly sank the boat. One thing's for certain, Jesus wasn't conventional.

He never seemed to do things the way people expected but then again, He was God's Son. But here's the odd story I want to tell you about. Jesus was for ever getting harassed by the religious leaders who didn't like His way of doing things one little bit. If they could just find some way to ruin His reputation then nobody would want to hear what Jesus had to say and they would be centre stage once again.

One of the ways these sneaky religious leaders tried to trip Jesus up was by attempting to trick Him into breaking one of their religious laws. Jesus and His disciples had just rocked up in a place called Capernaum and Peter was confronted by a religious official who wanted to know if Jesus obeyed the Jewish law by paying their temple tax. A good question. I suppose that Jesus could have turned around and said that because He was God's Son He didn't have to pay the tax, but Jesus told Peter that He wasn't in the business of stirring things up so He'd stump up.

To find out the odd way Jesus paid His tax go to Bible book Matthew, chapter 17 and verse 27.

The Israelite nation had been set free from slavery in Egypt and was now travelling through the desert towards a brand new homeland. If you know anything at all about deserts you'll be aware that they aren't exactly renowned for having lots of water. This uncomfortable fact was about to cause the Israelites a big, big problem.

But first let me tell you how God had taken care of these people so you don't end up giving Him a hard time like *they* did. It was God's idea to rescue the Israelites in the first place because He had a special plan for this nation. It was God who'd made a miraculous pathway through the Red Sea so that they could escape from Egypt. It was God who'd provided breakfast and dinner for them each and every day. (In the morning the desert floor was covered with a flake-like, sweet substance called manna and in the evening meat came in the form of flocks of quail birds being dispatched by God to where they were camped).

So, when one day the Israelites realised that they'd run out of water, did they shrug their shoulders and think to themselves, 'Why worry? God will sort us out with some water like He has with everything else.' Nope! They mumbled and grumbled that things had been much better for them back in Egypt. It might have been tough there but at least they didn't go thirsty. What an ungrateful lot, eh?

Moses (their leader) was well miffed with their ingratitude and went to ask God what to do. God told him to head over to a rock and, in full view of everyone, command water to come out of it. Moses was still fuming with rage because of the Israelites' grumbling and struck the rock twice with his wooden staff (which was a bit like a long walking stick) instead. As odd as it might seem, water gushed out of the rock and everyone had as much to drink as they wanted. Here's the rub. Moses hadn't spoken to the rock like God had told him.

ODD WAYS OF DOING THINGS NO.4

This next Bible bit is all about a very odd way a certain chap went about choosing a king for Israel. Often as not, when a new king is required it's the son of the previous king who gets the job. And the reason the new king is crowned is usually because the old one has pegged it (died).

In its early days, Israel didn't have a king. God wanted to be the One who led the Isaelites but they wouldn't take no for an answer. God finally gave in to their demands and Israel ended up with its first king, a guy called Saul.

After a reasonable start, Saul soon started to make a hash of things so God decided to replace Saul with a new king. I suppose God could have handed the job on to Saul's son (Jonathan) but He had other plans. God had His eye on a young lad who was off the radar as far as everyone else was concerned. The man that God sent to track down Israel's next king was Samuel. He was a bit of a hotshot in Israel and was the guy everyone looked up to when it came to hearing from God.

Samuel headed out to the town of Bethlehem (yep, the same one from the Christmas carol) and rolled up at the home of a chap called Jesse (which is a man's name even though it sounds a bit girlie). Jesse had eight sons and seven of them were lined up in front of Samuel to see which one God had chosen for the job of king. One by one Samuel cast his eagle eye over them but none of them fitted the bill. When Samuel found out that Jesse had one more son (David, his youngest) he had him fetched from the fields where he was looking after the sheep. Surely God wasn't going to make a shepherd boy a king?

ODD WAYS OF DOING THINGS NO.5

We drop in on the Moabites just as they discover that the Israelite nation is passing through their land en route to a place called Canaan. So what's the problem? Well, along the way the Israelites had fought the odd battle or two with the inhabitants of other lands they were crossing and every time they'd won. With the Israelites now on their doorstep the Moabites were none too happy. In fact they were scared silly. They figured that if they didn't act quickly they'd be mincemeat.

So Balak (their king) had an idea. There was a guy called Balaam who seemed to know a thing or two about supernatural stuff. Maybe he could put a curse on the Israelite intruders to send them packing. King Balak sent some of his top bods to pay Balaam a visit and to persuade him (in exchange for a stash of cash) to do the dirty on Israel. Before Balaam gave his answer he thought it best to check out what Israel's God had to say on the matter so, while his visitors kipped down for the night, Balaam got in touch with Him.

God quickly made it clear that he was to have nothing to do with this pesky plan and next morning Balaam sent the men on their way. Before long another even more important delegation arrived bringing with them even more money to try and persuade Balaam to rain down curses on Israel.

It seemed like Balaam tried to get God to change His mind because he asked God a second time what he should do. You get the impression that God wasn't too pleased with Balaam's refusal to take 'No' for an answer and this time God told Balaam to go with the men, if he really wanted to.

As Balaam set off on his donkey an angel from God kept blocking the way. Balaam couldn't see the angel but the donkey could. As it tried to squeeze past the angel Balaam's foot got scraped against a wall. Balaam was livid but he was about to have the oddest surprise of his life.

IF THEY WANT TO CALL US DONKEYS STUBBORN THEN THAT'S WHAT I'LL BE!

Read about it in Bible book Numbers, chapter 22 and verses 26 to 35.

I n the Old Testament part of the Bible you come across people called prophets. Their job was to listen to God and then to tell everyone else what God was saying. Sometimes it was good news but often as not it was God's way of telling people to quit being so bad and start being good.

One of the big-name prophets was Elijah and he lived in Israel at the time of wicked King Ahab. Elijah was the guy who made the rain stop for over three years because of Ahab's wicked ways. Elijah didn't hang around to find out what Ahab thought of what he'd done. He hot-footed it as far from the furious king as his legs would carry him and then hid out of harm's way until it was time to end the drought.

For some of his exile God sent ravens to feed the fleeing fella (it doesn't bear thinking about) and for some of the time he was looked after by a kind widow in a place called Zarephath.

Which leads us rather neatly on to another of Elijah's claims to fame. When the widow's son suddenly died it was Elijah who brought the guy back to life again. Amazing or what? As far as most people at the time were concerned,

Elijah was a bit of an oddball so it would have been no surprise when he took on all 450 prophets of the god Baal in a contest to see whose God was the best. Elijah's God won the day after Elijah called down fire from heaven to sizzle up a sacrifice.

Want to find out if Elijah looked as odd as he acted? Look up Bible book 2 Kings, chapter 1 and verses 6 to 8.

ODD WAYS OF DOING THINGS NO.7

'You can't fit a quart into a pint pot', so says the popular adage. What does that mean? I'll tell you. Most of you know what a pint is but a quart is more than a pint. If you try to pour a quart of liquid into a pint-sized pot it'll spill over the top. It can't be done! But that's precisely what God did when He sent Jesus into this world. Let me explain.

God's home isn't in our universe. He lives outside of it. You can't see where God lives but take my word for it (or more importantly, take the Bible's word for it) it exists. It was from there that God thought up the idea of creating the universe and everything in it in the first place so it's much, much bigger than anything you could imagine. Not only is where God lives mahoosive, but so is God Himself. The Bible says that God is everywhere and that He also fills everywhere, which is absolutely mind-blowing when you think about it.

So try to imagine God squeezing Himself into the size of a human being. Sounds impossible, doesn't it? But when God sent Jesus (His one and only Son) to earth to take the punishment for all the bad things we've done, the first thing

He had to do was to be born as a human being. Most of us know the Christmas story of how a young lady called Mary became pregnant with God's Son, but how many of us try to get our head around what that really means? A mega-sized God living in a man-sized body. How mind-boggling is that?

ODD WAYS OF DOING THINGS NO.8

When you go to school you can be sure of two things. One: you'll be taught lots and lots of stuff. Two: you'll be tested on what you've learned. It's only when you sit a test that you know what you've remembered, and what you've forgotten.

When Jesus came to live on the earth around 2,000 years ago He came as God but He also had a human body. Jesus was on a mission to get people back to being friends with God and to do that He was going to give His life as a sacrifice that would pay the price for all the wrong things people do. To do *that*, Jesus had to be perfect as a human being as well as being perfect as God (which He was). From the moment Jesus was born He lived a tip-top life and didn't put a foot wrong. He could only do that because of God's life in Him. Jesus has an enemy who goes by the name of Satan (or the devil) who knew full well who Jesus was and wasted no time in seeing if he could try to make God's Son slip up and do something bad. It was showdown time and Jesus went out into the desert to meet His archenemy. If Satan could tempt

Jesus to use His God-power in a wrong way then He wouldn't be able to finish His mission from God. Having failed miserably to goad Jesus into turning the rocks into bread (Jesus hadn't eaten for forty days) and leaping off the highest building in Jerusalem to see if God caught Him, Satan had one final trick up his sleeve.

You can read all about it in Bible book Matthew, chapter 4 and verses 8 to 11.

Let me introduce you to King Solomon of Israel who was as wise as wise can be. Not only did he speak with great wisdom but he also wrote loads and loads of wise things as well. What a clever chap he was. In fact there is a whole Bible book that is crammed full with Solomon's wise words. It's called Proverbs and although a few other guys chipped in and wrote some stuff, King Solomon generally gets the credit for writing the lion's share.

Rather than having to wade through the entire thirty-one books in Proverbs yourself I have come to the rescue and have cherry-picked some of the more juicy gems (in my humble opinion) for you to enjoy. In no particular order, how about *this* profound proverb for starters: 'A wise son pays attention when his father corrects him, but an arrogant person never admits he is wrong.' You might not like the sound of this one if you're a kid (and if you're not, what on earth are you doing taking a sneaky look at a children's book?) but I'll bet that this comes right near the top of the list for most mums and dads! For your info it's from Bible book Proverbs, chapter 13 and it's the very first verse.

If you've ever had a row with someone then you'll know how hard it is to stop once you've started. Nobody wants to back down even if they know they're in the wrong, do they? I guess that the best way to avoid an argument getting out of hand is to stop it in its tracks before it builds up a head of steam.

No surprises that Solomon has some wise words to say about this tricky situation. 'The start of an argument is like the first break in a dam; stop it before it goes any further.' You can find this one in Bible book Proverbs, chapter 17 and verse 14. Now here's one for you to finish off. 'Stupid people always think they are right ...'

You can find the rest of it in Bible book Proverbs, chapter 12 and verse 15.

16
PICK OF THE PROVERBS NO.2

King Solomon, the fella who wrote the sayings or proverbs that we're going to look at next, seemed to have had a bit of a problem in the domestic bliss department. What I mean by that is his wife appeared to be giving him more than his fair share of grief.

First let's see what Solomon had to say and then we can try and find out what was going on behind closed doors. In Bible book Proverbs, chapter 21 and verse 9 the king bares his soul with this heartfelt saying: 'Better to live on the roof than share the house with a nagging wife.' Oh dear. That doesn't sound good. Not content with that, a few verses later (in verse 19) Solomon lets rip with, 'Better to live out in the desert than with a nagging, complaining wife.' What on earth is going on between him and wifey?

Well, we won't find out quite yet because in Proverbs chapter 27 and verse 15 King Solomon adds the following piece of wisdom to his list of wifely woes: 'A nagging wife is like water going drip-drip-drip on a rainy day.' Now before you begin to feel sorry for King Solomon I need to fill you in on a thing or two about the guy.

Solomon (Israel's king at the time) didn't have one wife (as people normally do) but a staggering 700! Imagine listening to that many wives. But then again, if you were just one among so many I guess you might have cause for feeling a bit cheesed off every now and then for not getting your hubby's full attention. King Solomon's wives were eventually his downfall.

PICK OF THE PROVERBS NO.3

A well-known saying that *doesn't* feature in the Bible goes like this: 'Sticks and stones may break my bones but names will never hurt me.' Anyone who's been on the receiving end of some nasty words knows that this is not true. Words can hurt us which means that words are powerful.

The Bible makes this point over and over again. Right at the beginning of time God gave the command and the world and the whole universe sprang into being. How awesome is that? So it should come as no surprise to us that there are loads and loads of proverbs to do with what comes out of our mouths. Later on in the Bible (in Matthew, chapter 15 and verse 18) it says that, '...the things that come out of the mouth come from the heart ...' That means if you're a good person then good stuff will come out. But if you're not so nice then the chances are you'll be the sort of person who says not very nice things.

Here's a Bible proverb which talks about this. 'Kind words bring life, but cruel words crush your spirit.' Kind words can be like good medicine and as we know, medicine usually makes us feel better. You can find that wise saying in Proverbs

chapter 15 and verse 4. So that's an encouragement from King Solomon (the writer of this proverb) to speak kind words to other people, and hopefully they'll do the same to us.

Sometimes it's not so much what we say as what we don't say. Who knows that it's really hard not to spill the beans when you know something bad about somebody? It's called gossip and spreading rumours about people or sharing something that was told to you in private can cause a whole heap of harm. Here's some handy advice from the book of Proverbs about this. 'No one who gossips can be trusted with a secret, but you can put confidence in someone who is trustworthy.' You'll find that in chapter 11 and verse 13. Wise words indeed!

Want some help in keeping your mouth shut when you need to? Bible book Psalms, chapter 141 and verse 3 has got a prayer that will help you.

PICK OF THE PROVERBS NO.4

'The devil makes work for idle hands' or so goes the popular saying. The Bible talks a lot about the devil, mainly because he's God's No.1 enemy. Just to let you know, the devil is most definitely not powerful like God. He just likes to *think* he is. And one thing that the devil's a big fan of is laziness. Why's that? Because the devil knows full well that laziness is a downward slope to ruin, and spoiling people's lives is his speciality.

God, on the other hand, doesn't share the devil's love of wasting your days doing nothing. God's a big fan of everyone chipping in and doing what they can to make the world a better place. There are a number of proverbs about being bone idle and we're going to check out a few of them now.

For starters in Bible book Proverbs, chapter 19 and verse 15 it says, 'Be lazy if you want to; sleep on, but you will go hungry'. In other words if you can't be bothered to get out of bed and look for work then you'll go hungry and have yourself to blame. Then there's this one: 'A farmer who is too lazy to plough his fields at the right time will have nothing to harvest'

(Proverbs chapter 20 and verse 4). Any sensible farmer would agree with that. Or then again how about, 'Never get a lazy person to do something for you; he will be as irritating as vinegar on your teeth or smoke in your eyes', from Proverbs chapter 10 and verse 26. In other words, working alongside someone who won't lift a finger to help is no fun.

But the Bible also offers a spot of practical help on how not to be lazy. In Proverbs chapter 6 and verse 6 we are told that a certain hard working insect can be an example to us all. 'Lazy people should learn a lesson from the way ants live.' Ants always seem to be busy, working away at their anthills and carrying bits and bobs to and fro to build them. That's the sort of hard work that gets results and which lounging around in bed all day won't.

To find out one big advantage of not being lazy head for Bible book Proverbs, chapter 10 and verse 4.

19

PICK OF THE PROVERBS NO.5

or our last look at the wise sayings of King Solomon I thought I'd pick out a few of the odder ones. Throughout Bible book Proverbs it compares people who have wisdom (like Solomon) with people who don't. The Bible calls them fools or foolish. So if you're one of the wise ones you'll make good decisions. If, on the other hand, you're a fool then the chances are you'll keep on making bad decisions.

As if to prove the point, Bible book Proverbs, chapter 26 and verse 11 informs us that, 'A fool doing some stupid thing a second time is like a dog going back to its vomit'. Yuk! Sounds revolting, but it gets the message across that without wisdom a person will probably keep on doing the same old silly things. Later on in the Bible, a chap called Peter quotes this very proverb when talking about people who make Jesus No.1 in their lives and then change their minds and go back to living their old selfish lives. Peter also added another saying that's not in the book of Proverbs but it's a good 'un nonetheless – check out Bible book 2 Peter, chapter 2 and verse 22: 'A pig that has been washed goes back to roll in the mud.' In other words, they'll just keep returning to their foolish old ways.

Check out Proverbs chapter 17 and verse 12 and you'll soon discover that being a fool is not a joking matter. 'It is better to meet a mother bear robbed of her cubs than to meet some fool busy with a stupid project.' In other words, who knows what a person lacking wisdom will do next, so best not to hang around them just in case.

'A fool does not care whether he understands a thing or not; all he wants to do is to show how clever he is', is what it tells us in Proverbs chapter 18 and verse 2. Proverbs chapter 15 and verse 20 says that, 'Wise children make their fathers happy. Only fools despise their mothers'. And in chapter 14 and verse 29, 'If you stay calm, you are wise, but if you have a hot temper, you only show how stupid you are'.

So the big question is, how can you stop being a fool (if you are one)?

All is not lost! Bible book James, chapter 1 and verse 5 has your answer.

DOUBLE ACTS NO.1

There are a fair few double acts that crop up in the Bible such as Mary and Joseph (Jesus' mum and dad), Moses and Aaron (the two brothers whom God used to rescue the Israelite nation from slavery in Egypt) and not forgetting the world's very first human twosome, Adam and Eve. The pair of them both had an unusual start to life. Adam was created from dirt (by God) and then came to life when God breathed into him. Eve, on the other hand, was made out of a rib which God removed from Adam's chest while he slept.

God had given Adam and Eve strict instructions to fill the world with people who would look after it for Him. Did that mean that God would have to make some more mud men or rib ladies? No it didn't. It was time for Eve to give birth to the world's first baby. He was formed inside his mum just like every other human being has been from that day to this. Adam and Eve's first kid was called Cain and when he grew up he farmed the land. Their second child was also a boy and they named him Abel.

Abel grew up to be a sheep farmer. Although the brothers' mum and dad did something bad that spoiled their relationship with God, the lines of communication were still open to Him.

Which is why as we catch up with Cain and Abel, they're about to offer sacrifices to God. Cain presented some crops from his harvest to God and Abel offered God the first-born lamb of one of his sheep.

It's not completely clear why, but God gave Abel a well-deserved pat on the back for his offering but was less than pleased with what Cain brought. Cain was well-miffed and decided to take revenge on his younger brother. What I *will* tell you is that very soon this brotherly double act was no more, but the rest of this gory story you'll have to find out for yourself.

Head for Bible book Genesis, chapter 4 and verse 8 for all the gory details.

DOUBLE ACTS NO.2

The next Bible double act we're putting under the spotlight is Deborah and Barak. In case you were wondering, they weren't a husband and wife team like Adam and Eve. Deborah was one of the rulers of Israel and Barak was her military commander.

For your information, Israel's rulers at that time were called judges. The Israelites had finally settled in the land of Canaan after escaping from slavery in Egypt and these judges kept them on the right track with God and also led them into war against their enemies. All in all, there were at least twelve leaders whom the Bible calls judges. Deborah was judge number four and she'd come on the scene after Israel had been conquered by the Canaanite king, Jabin of Hazor.

Jabin had given the Israelites a hard time but it was their own fault. They'd turned their backs on God and as a result things had gone from bad to worse ending up with twenty years of misery under this Canaanite king. The Israelites cried out to God and being the kind God that He is, God came to the rescue, or rather He raised up Deborah to lead them to victory.

The feisty female judge summoned Barak and told him that God had given her a strategy to overthrow King Jabin.

Barak was to take 10'000 fighting men to meet Sisera (Jabin's military commander) and trick him into coming out to fight. God promised that the Canaanite army would be defeated but Barak wouldn't go into battle without Deborah. Was he a wuss? Who knows? But because of this Deborah declared that he wasn't going to get any of the credit for winning the war. That would go to a woman. Did this really happen?

Check out how the story ends in Bible book Judges, chapter 4 and verses 15 to 24.

DOUBLE ACTS NO.3

Paul and Barnabas were a dynamic duo who feature a lot in Bible book Acts (or The Acts of the Apostles). It was called this because it's action-packed with tales of what Jesus' disciples got up to after He'd gone back to heaven. Just so you know, Paul originally went by the name of Saul and if you're observant you'll notice that his name changes to Paul in chapter 13 of Bible book Acts. As for Barnabas (whose name means 'encourager'), we first get wind of him early on in the book of Acts when he sells a plot of land he owns and gives the money to the church. How kind of him.

This Bible double act were now hanging out in a place called Antioch where they were part of the church. There was so much to do that Barnabas and his fellow leaders needed a helping hand. Barnabas had made a special trip to go and fetch Paul from a place called Tarsus and then bring him back to Antioch to help out. God was doing great things and it was all hands to the pump. Paul and Barnabas were a pair of hot shots for God and they were now raring to travel the world telling more and more people about Jesus.

They didn't have long to wait to get their marching orders. During one of their church meetings the Holy

Spirit gave them the green light to pack their bags and to get on with things. Although Paul and Barnabas were Jews by birth they were planning to take the good news, that Jesus had made it possible to be friends with God, to the non-Jews (or Gentiles) as well.

Everyone gathered round Paul and Barnabas, they placed their hands on this tip-top twosome, and sent them off with their blessing. Did this double act always stay best buddies?

You'll find the answer in Bible book Acts, chapter 15 and verses 36 to 41.

DOUBLE ACTS NO.4

There's only one way to describe this Bible double act and that's 'double trouble'. As you are about to discover, these twin boys were as bad as each other. Their mum and dad (Isaac and Rebekah) were getting on a bit and after twenty years of married life Rebekah finally gave birth. Even before the lads popped out, their mum knew trouble was brewing.

She had a chat to God about why being pregnant was such hard work and God came back with a surprise answer. First off, she wasn't carrying one baby, but two. Secondly, God gave Rebekah the heads-up that her twin boys were actually squabbling inside her (and that wouldn't change when they were born). They'd continue to be at each others' throats throughout their lives and that was that. To make matters worse, God said that her younger son (Jacob) would become the top dog in the family and not her elder son (Esau).

Even on the day of their birth Jacob could be seen grabbing on tight to Esau's heel as they emerged. Years later, when the pair had grown up, Jacob was still on the lookout for what he could grab from his big brother. One day Esau returned from a spot of hunting and was absolutely famished. Crafty Jacob offered his brother some of his homemade stew in exchange for Esau's right to be head of the household (and everything that went with it) when their dad died. Hungry Esau foolishly agreed to his kid brother's demands.

Although parents shouldn't have favourites, Esau was most definitely Isaac's blue-eyed boy. As for Rebekah, well, Jacob was her ray of sunshine. Isaac was getting on in years and figured that his days were numbered. Isaac was keen to make sure he passed on his special blessing (from God) to Esau so that at least his eldest lad had *something* when he was gone. But Jacob had his eyes on that as well. With the help of his mum, Jacob tricked his dad (whose eyesight was failing) into placing his hand on him (thinking he was Esau) so that *he* got the special blessing instead.

No prizes for guessing that Esau was hopping mad when he found out and Jacob ran for the hills. Did the two ever patch things up?

Find out in Bible book Genesis, chapter 33 and verses 1 to 4.

24

DOUBLE ACTS NO.5

Have you ever been to a show where the star is off sick and the understudy gets the chance to go centre stage for the night? Well, the next Bible double act was a bit like that. King Saul (who for your information was Israel's very first king) had been making a wee bit of a hash of ruling God's special nation and God had decided to call time on his antics. Waiting in the wings was a young lad called David, whom God had lined up to replace him.

But David wasn't going to take the limelight for just one show. He was going to give Saul the elbow and take his place permanently. King Saul wasn't planning to go quietly though. He rather enjoyed being top of the bill and it would be over his dead body that this young upstart David would nick his crown. When David won a great victory for the Israelites everyone was talking about this amazing young shepherd boy from Bethlehem. When Saul found out about David's ever-increasing popularity he was livid, and determined to kill him before he got anywhere near Israel's throne.

The conniving king tried to skewer David with a spear but David managed to escape and did a runner. Saul sent his troops on the warpath to track down David and things nearly went

belly-up when David found himself with a golden opportunity to take out his tormentor once and for all. But David respected God too much to kill a man whom God had made king (even though Saul had fouled up).

In the end, King Saul was killed in battle and at long last David could be crowned king of Israel. Why did God choose David to be king?

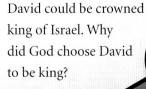

Take a look in Bible book Acts, chapter 13 and verse 22.

25

DOUBLE ACTS NO.6

Have you ever played that game where someone gives you a word and then you have to say the first thing that pops into your head? For instance, if I said 'salt' you would probably say 'pepper'. If I said 'knife' you'd say 'fork' and if I said 'cat' there's a good possibility you'd say 'dog'. So when it comes to Bible characters, if I say 'David' there's every chance you're going to reply 'Goliath'. Maybe I'm right, maybe I'm wrong, but it's a fact that these two are one of the most famous double acts in the Bible and it's this pair we're going to take a look at now.

Take a look through the Old Testament part of the Bible and you'll not take long to find a story of some nation or other going to war against Israel. One enemy who seemed to take more than their fair share of pot-shots against the Israelites were the Philistines. Sometimes they'd win and sometimes they'd lose, but the Bible bit we're about to look at now has the Philistines starting out with a ginormous advantage.

They had a secret weapon that they'd brought out onto the battlefield and it was scaring the Israelite army silly. What was this weapon? It was a fella called Goliath. So what was the problem? Just the small matter (or should I say BIG matter)

of Goliath's size. This Philistine warrior checked in at over nine feet tall and was literally head and shoulders above any of the Israelites' finest fighters. Goliath was having a field day taunting the Israelites to come and take him on. Gulp! No way! It would have remained stalemate if a young chap called David hadn't rocked up to the battlefield to deliver packed lunches for his brothers (who were in the army).

Want to find out how long David and Goliath lasted as a Bible double act?

Head for Bible book 1 Samuel, chapter 17 and verses 41 to 51.

26

DOUBLE ACTS NO.7

I t's great when you have nice neighbours where you live but not much fun if you've got bad ones. That was the lot of poor, unfortunate Naboth. One of his near neighbours was none other than Ahab, the wicked king of Israel. Along with his wife, Jezebel the pair of them were double trouble and made life miserable for Israel's inhabitants.

Ahab had his eye on Naboth's vineyard which he wanted to turn into a vegetable patch for his palace. King Ahab offered his neighbour the going rate for the vineyard but Naboth wasn't interested. It had been in his family for donkey's years and he was in no mood to sell it. Ahab went off back to his palace angry and depressed because he hadn't been able to get his own way.

His wife, Jezebel soon put a stop to all that. She told him to quit sulking and to snap out of it. Jezebel reminded her hubbie that he was king and could do whatever he wanted. That included getting his hands on Naboth's vineyard whether Naboth liked it or not. Jezebel hatched a sneaky plan to call together the leaders of the town and to accuse Naboth of speaking out against God.

It wasn't true, but that didn't seem to matter. Naboth was stoned to death as a punishment for this concocted crime and Ahab was free to nab the vineyard.

Just one thing. God had been watching all along and He was none too pleased with what He'd seen. God sent one of His prophets to inform Ahab that his days were now numbered. In the very place where the innocent Naboth had met his end, King Ahab would also die and his blood would be licked up by dogs.

Yucky yoo! Did the vineyard-grabbing king get his comeuppance like the prophet said?

For the next Bible double act I'm also going to give you *double* the double acts, which means we'll be looking at not two, but four people. First up we have a young guy called Samuel and a priest called Eli. After that I'm going to introduce you to Eli's two sons called Hophni and Phineas.

Eli was the main man in Israel at this time and he ran the show from a place called Shiloh. This was the base for all worship and sacrifice to God in the nation and it was where Samuel ended up us a young lad. Samuel's mum had dedicated him to God before he was born and now Eli was responsible for his upbringing.

Although Eli appeared to be doing quite a good job of looking after Samuel and keeping him on the straight and narrow, the same could not be said of Eli's own sons, Hophni and Phineas. They also worked at Israel's place of worship but the Bible makes it pretty clear that they didn't take their job seriously. God was well aware that they were misusing their authority and position and it was something that He was not prepared to tolerate one moment longer.

To be fair to Eli, he'd had words with his boys to try and persuade them to turn over a new leaf but it was a little late in

the day for that. God sent along one of his prophets to break
the news to Eli that because he'd allowed the place of worship
to be overrun with wickedness, every member of his family
would die young. To make it absolutely clear that what God
had said would happen the prophet went on to say that Hophni
and Phineas would meet their end on the very same day.

Find out if this happened
in Bible book 1 Samuel,
chapter 4 and verses
1 to 11.

DOUBLE ACTS NO.9

My guess is that one of the most well-known twosomes in the Bible is none other than Mary and Joseph (Jesus' mum and dad). One reason for that is that they show up every year at Christmas time in nativity plays, on Christmas cards and in Christmas carols. Now that's what I call being a celebrity!

Not that this was something the pair of them ever sought. Mary was just an ordinary gal living in an ordinary place called Nazareth but she was about to have an extraordinary experience that would change her life in an extraordinary way. An angel from God (who went by the name of Gabriel) dropped in, unannounced, and told Mary that she was going to give birth to a Son who would be from God.

It was one thing finding she was pregnant but another thing having to break the news to her fiancé (Joseph). Rather than kick up a fuss Joseph offered to quietly call off the wedding, but not before God had sent an angel to him as well. While Joseph was fast asleep the angel appeared to him in a dream and told him that the baby was God's and not another man's. Phew, that was a relief to him. Without further ado Joseph took the bull by the horns and promised to marry Mary.

Mary and Joseph feature as a double act a few more times in the Bible. There's that famous trip to Bethlehem where Mary gives birth and they then get a surprise visit from those famous shepherds. A bit later on those equally famous wise men also roll up to pay their respects to this special child. A little later Mary and Joseph hot-foot it to Egypt to protect their lad from being killed by Israel's horrid Herod who thought that Jesus was after his crown.

Want to read up about the last time Mary and Joseph appear as a double act?

Make tracks for Bible book Luke, chapter 2 and verses 41 to 52.

The next Bible double act we're shining the spotlight on would almost certainly feature on Santa's 'Naughty List'. They went by the name of Herod and Herodias and they were definitely a couple of Bible baddies. Boo, hiss! Herod was simply the name that the ruling family in Israel took and the Herod who features in this Bible bit was one of a few.

The whole Herod family probably had a bit of a chip on their shoulder because they weren't free to do completely as they pleased. They were 'puppet kings' which meant that they were answerable to the Roman rulers of Israel. Because of their lavish lifestyle and because of their cruelty, the Herods weren't really a big hit with inhabitants of Israel.

When a guy called John the Baptist (that wasn't his surname, it's just how he's become known) shot to fame because of his outlandish ways and his message that it was time people turned back to God, Herod's ears pricked up. Herod was intrigued and wanted to hear more. I'm not sure why, because John was very outspoken about Herod's wicked ways. Maybe Herod wanted to turn over a new leaf. Who knows? Anyway, the rotten ruler didn't have to wait long for his chance. John told Herod that he was wrong to marry his brother's wife, Herodias. Herodias was livid and had John arrested and flung into prison.

To be fair to Herod, he did sort of respect John the Baptist and wanted to understand what he was saying about God. Herodias on the other hand wanted the oddball preacher out of her hair as quickly as possible and Herod's birthday bash proved the ideal opportunity. Her daughter captivated Herod with her dazzling dance routine and Herod foolishly promised her anything she wanted – even up to half the kingdom!

30

DOUBLE ACTS NO.11

I f I were to mention the name of Joshua to you there's every chance you might remember him as being the guy who led the Israelites around the city of Jericho for seven days before God brought its walls tumbling down. Well, for this Bible double acts bit we're going to link him up with a chap called Caleb who there's every chance you've probably never heard of.

The story I'm going to tell you happened many, many years before Joshua's famous Jericho escapade and stars not just these two guys but ten others as well. They'd been sent by their leader, Moses as undercover agents to sneak into Canaan and to spy out the land. God had lined up Canaan for the Israelite nation to settle down in, but God had instructed Moses to send in spies first to check out what the land was like and find out what sort of opposition they might meet.

After a forty day foray into Canaan the spies returned safely with some good news and some bad news. The good news was that the land was fertile, lush and brimming over with yummy crops. To prove it they lugged back a humongous bunch of grapes (it took two men to carry it on a pole), figs and pomegranates. What were they waiting for? Canaan was theirs for the taking.

Er, not so fast. The land might have been choc-a-block full of fabulous fruit but the bad news was that it was also home to some rather ginormous people. Scary or what! No way were they going into Canaan if it meant having to fight that lot. All of the spies (except for Joshua and Caleb) were dead set against entering the place. Having been scared silly by their terrifying tales, the rest of the Israelites were in agreement.

Sad to say, the courageous couple of Caleb and Joshua would have to wait another forty years before they finally got into Canaan. But what became of all those scaredy cats?

31

DOUBLE ACTS NO.12

Did you know that Moses had a brother and sister called Aaron and Miriam? They'd been brought up with the other Israelite slaves in Egypt while Moses had fallen on his feet and had got raised in Pharaoh's palace. Years later the three of them were reunited when God used Moses to set the Israelites free from captivity.

First Aaron was reunited with his long lost kid brother and the two of them joined forces to try and convince the Pharaoh to release the Israelites. Aaron became Moses' right hand man and got to see first-hand the mighty miracles God performed for his brother. Miriam got to see what a hotshot Moses was for God when her brother stretched out his wooden staff over the Red Sea and the waters parted creating a pathway for the entire Israelite nation to cross through. How proud they must have been that Moses was their own flesh and blood.

Unfortunately the novelty of being free quickly wore off and the pair of them started grumbling and complaining because Moses had gone and married an Ethiopian woman. Whatever the reason was, they had a mahoosive problem with this and began to have second thoughts about whether Moses should be the Israelites' main man after all. They reasoned that

because Moses wasn't the only one who heard from God then what right did *he* have to be in charge.

This jaded duo had made a big mistake by speaking out against God's appointed leader. God had eavesdropped on every word and told them to meet up with Moses at the Tabernacle tent where God was worshipped. God told the two of them that they were well out of order for criticising Moses and when God left, Miriam suddenly discovered that she was covered in a dreaded skin disease called leprosy.

See how the story ends in Bible book Numbers, chapter 12 and verses 13 to 16.

Lots of people have heard of a guy from the Bible called Samson. He was known for his great strength and for his long hair. But Samson was also part of a Bible double act along with a gal called Delilah. Let me quickly give you a bit of background to them and then we'll head for the grand finale of their lives together.

The Israelites were taking a bit of a pounding from their old enemy the Philistines. It was their own fault. They'd strayed far from the God whom they were supposed to worship and this was their punishment. It was God's way of making them aware of their failings so that they'd turn back to Him. Once the Israelites had learned their lesson, God's plan was to rescue them. That's where Samson comes in.

Samson's mum and dad hadn't been able to have any kids but that was about to change. The perplexed pair had a surprise visit from an angel who informed them that they were going to have a son, but that wasn't all. This lad would belong to God and he wasn't to drink alcohol or to have his hair cut – ever! Their son's name was Samson and his mum and dad obeyed God's instructions.

As Samson grew up it soon become clear that there was something special about him. One day Samson discovered this for himself when he was attacked by a ferocious lion. God's Spirit came upon Samson and gave him superhuman strength to kill the lion and tear it to shreds. Awesome!

Samson used his God-given power to attack the Philistines and to begin to release the Israelites from their grip. When Samson fell head over heels in love with Delilah the Philistines saw a chance to rid themselves of Israel's strongman. They bribed Delilah into finding out the secret of her boyfriend's strength. After loads of nagging Samson finally gave in and spilled the beans.

Find out what became of Samson in Bible book Judges, chapter 16 and verses 17 to 31.

33

DOUBLE ACTS NO.14

Our last Bible double act is Ruth and Naomi. As you will soon discover, it could have very well nearly been a triple act, and that would have meant none of them would have featured in this book. The good news is (for Ruth and Naomi) that's not what happened. Here's the story in a nutshell.

Naomi and her hubbie (Elimelech) emigrated from Israel to Moab because of a famine in their land. They had a couple of boys called Mahlon and Chilion who also went with them. Sad to say, Elimelech never made it back to Israel. He died in Moab. In the meantime Naomi's sons got hitched (married) to a couple of local lasses (Ruth and Orpah). Things were looking up again. But not for long. Who'd have believed it, but Mahlon and Chilion went the way of their dad and also died. What a disaster!

Naomi had a ponder about what to do and decided that there was nothing for it but to go back to Israel. News had reached her that the famine was over so the decision was made. Ruth and Orpah bawled their eyes out at the thought of Naomi leaving. They didn't want their mother-in-law to go. But go she must. Naomi told them to stay in Moab where they'd have a better chance of getting married again.

Orpah went along with Naomi's suggestion but Ruth had other ideas. She planned to stick with her mother-in-law through thick and thin, whatever lay ahead. That wasn't all. Ruth was determined to continue worshipping the same God as Naomi and going with her to Israel would help in that. Ruth and Naomi had a good old cry, waved Orpah goodbye and made tracks for their new life in Israel.

You'll be pleased to know that this Bible double act had a happy ending. Ruth found herself a new hubbie and Naomi finally had a grandson whom they called Obed. Obed eventually became the granddad of a very famous Bible king.

To find out who it was head to Bible book Ruth, chapter 4 and verses 13 to 17.

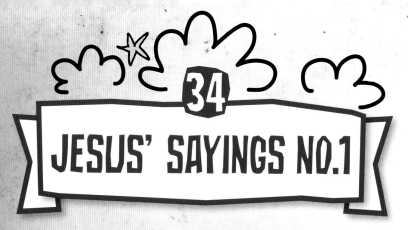

34

JESUS' SAYINGS NO.1

Jesus is famous for a number of things such as healing the sick, bringing some fortunate folk back to life (after they'd died) and doing some amazing miracles like feeding 5,000 people with just a young lad's packed lunch.

But Jesus also spent a lot of His time teaching. I'm not talking about the sort of things you learn at school like two plus two equals four (I hope that's the right answer) and what the capital of France is (and don't say 'F'). The sort of things that Jesus taught people about were what God is like, how much He loves us and how we can be best of buddies with God. Jesus used expressions or sayings to help His listeners understand what He was driving at and to help them remember what He said.

I guess it must have worked because around 2,000 years later we're still using some of these unusual sayings. So how about we take a look at some of them and find out what they mean. The first one we're going to dive into is this: 'The blind leading the blind', which is whipped from Bible book Matthew, chapter 15 and verse 14. What's that all about? I'll tell you.

The Jewish religious leaders in Jesus' time were doing a pretty rubbish job of teaching people about God. As far as

Jesus was concerned, they knew far less than they thought about God which meant that they weren't really qualified for the job. These spiritual leaders didn't understand (or see) things the way God did. According to Jesus this made them spiritually blind.

So what you had was a nation of people who knew little about God being led by a bunch of leaders who knew little about God. That was a recipe for disaster just as it would be if a real blind person was trying to lead another blind person around.

Want to find out another expression Jesus used to describe the religious leaders?

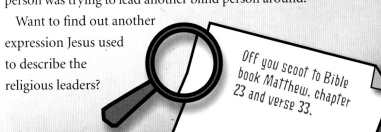

Off you scoot to Bible book Matthew, chapter 23 and verse 33.

35

JESUS' SAYINGS NO.2

For as long as most Jews could remember, their nation had been forbidden by God to eat certain foods. Some of it was to do with hygiene and cleanliness so that they didn't tuck into meat that would give them a squiffy tummy (or worse). And some of it was to do with simply learning to be obedient to God and to do what He said, when He said it.

One of the things that the Jews were forbidden to eat was pork (which was obviously jolly good news for pigs). Pigs have a bit of a reputation for being human dustbins and scoffing up just about anything that they can chomp on. Which is why they also have a reputation for being mucky pups (or should I say, pigs). Chuck them all your rotten old leftovers and rubbish and they'll be as happy as can be. But serve them up a three course gourmet meal cooked by the world's finest chef and your average pig wouldn't know the difference between it and a pile of soggy cabbage leaves.

So when Jesus was talking to a crowd of people about some of the things that were important to God and He told 'em, 'Do not throw your pearls in front of pigs – they will only trample them underfoot', His message came across loud and clear. You can find it in Bible book Matthew, chapter 7 and verse 6. What did that saying mean? Simple. Not everybody wants to listen to the wonderful things that you know about God. They might be really precious and valuable to you but to someone else who couldn't care less about God they'll be wasted words or like rubbish given to pigs.

The Bible has more to say about spending too much time in the company of people who have no time for God.

I'LL HAVE THE SWILL, PLEASE!

Menu

Check it out in Bible book 2 Corinthians. chapter 6 and verse 14.

At the time when Jesus was saying all these things the nation of Israel (where He lived) was under the thumb of the Romans. The Roman Empire had spread far and wide, including the land of Israel. Being invaded isn't the nicest of things and the inhabitants of Israel (the Jews) were well-miffed about the way things had turned out. The sooner that the Romans were gone the better as far as they were concerned.

It really didn't help that as well as paying taxes to them the Jewish people had to do what they were told by these rotten Roman rulers. Roman soldiers were actually allowed to stop you in the street and force you to carry their bag, which seems a bit unfair, but that's just the way it was. On the plus side, they could only ask you to carry it for a mile. After that you were free to hand the bag back and to go your own way.

Jesus used this particular Roman law to teach the Jewish people a valuable lesson. 'If a soldier forces you to carry his pack one mile, carry it two miles,' was what Jesus told them. Hang on a minute, that can't be right, can it? Yep, it can. Jesus wanted the Jewish people (and us) to know that God doesn't want people to begrudgingly do just the bare minimum. He wants us to give our heart and soul to everything we do, especially when it comes to our enemies (like the Romans).

The expression that has been coined for this is 'to go the extra mile'. You can check out this saying of Jesus in Bible book Matthew, chapter 5 and verse 41.

Just so you don't think that Jesus was making things hard for them, don't forget that He also went the extra mile when He came to earth (from heaven) to take the punishment for all the bad stuff that we do. Because He loves us, Jesus did far more than He ever needed to.

37

JESUS' SAYINGS NO.4

Jesus often taught the crowds who followed Him around stories (or parables, as they were called) to help them understand what God is like and how He expects people to live. One of the most well-known parables stars a Jewish chap who was making a trip from Jerusalem to Jericho.

It probably wasn't the wisest decision to make (going on his own) because the road he was taking was a haunt for robbers and rogues who lay in wait for unsuspecting travellers, but maybe he had no choice. Anyway, off he set and sure enough, before very long, the poor fellow fell victim to a gang of thieves and was attacked, robbed and left for dead. Boo hoo! Fear not, the story isn't over quite yet. We've got to get a popular saying into this first.

For all its lurking dangers the road to Jericho was obviously quite well used because the Bible tells us that before very long a Jewish priest came by. Phew, that's a relief! Help is at hand. Er, no it isn't. The priest side-stepped the mugged man and just kept on walking as if nothing was amiss. He wasn't alone in his actions. A Levite (a guy who helped in Jerusalem's temple) did the very same thing.

Just when it seemed like all hope was lost, along came a man from Samaria. The Jews and the Samaritans (as they were called) didn't really hit it off so it came as a big surprise when Jesus announced that this enemy was the one who actually took care of the beaten-up bloke.

Which is why we call people who are kind and helpful (like the guy in the story) a 'good Samaritan'. Jesus had one more thing to say to His listeners and to us also.

See what it was in Bible book Luke, chapter 10 and verses 36 and 37.

38

JESUS' SAYINGS NO.5

Some of the sayings that Jesus used, such as 'don't hide your light under a bushel', can sound a little bit weird. To understand this particular saying it would be handy to know what a bushel actually is so that we can then avoid hiding our light under it.

In the olden days a bushel was a measurement of weight. It was used for weighing things like grain and was equivalent to four pecks. That probably doesn't help you very much, does it, 'cos my guess is that you've not a clue what a peck is either, have you? So let me tell you that a peck is equivalent to eight quarts. Is that clearer? Probably not. I'm bamboozling you with all those ancient weights and measures, aren't I? Okay so here's a better way of explaining this. Imagine approximately eighteen bottles of lemonade (those big two litre-sized ones you have for parties). Find a container large enough to hold it all and that's what a bushel size looks like. We got there eventually, didn't we?

But although we now know how big a bushel container is, that still doesn't really help us to understand what Jesus' strange saying means. In Bible book Matthew, chapter 5 Jesus had been talking about how His disciples ought to point people to God.

He'd been saying that they should be like salt in the world. Salt often improves the flavour of food and so His followers should also bring the best out of the world they live in. Jesus then went on to say that His followers were to allow the life that God had given them to shine out brightly like a light and not to keep it hidden (or under a bushel).

To find out why we should do this look up Bible book Matthew, chapter 5 and verse 16.

39

JESUS' SAYINGS NO.6

One of Jesus' sayings that a lot of people know is 'I am the way, the truth and the life'. Jesus went on to say that nobody could become friends with God (His Father in heaven) unless He was involved. Why did Jesus say that? Because there were (and always will be) plenty of people around who'd like us to think that they can get us connected with God if we'll just do things their way. Sometimes people like that can be just a bit misguided and not really mean any harm. That's not always the case though and Jesus sent out a warning to be on our guard for people who sound like they have our best interests at heart but are only really interested in themselves. The expression Jesus coined to describe them was 'wolves in sheep's clothing'.

On the whole, sheep are pretty harmless and you've little to fear from them. A wolf, on the other hand, isn't quite so nice and friendly. Most of the children's stories that feature wolves paint these prowling creatures as mean and nasty and that's exactly the idea that Jesus is trying to get across.

Now imagine a wolf disguised as a sheep. Why on earth would a wolf do something like that? Easy peasy. According to Jesus it would be to trick someone into believing that they were harmless (like a sheep) but all the while they were out to deceive them and lead them away from God, without the person realising it.

You can find all of this in Bible book Matthew, chapter 7 and verse 15. Jesus also talked about sheep (and shepherds) when He wanted to show how much He cares for us.

40

HEADS-UP NO.1

You'll probably have noticed that in these books we're a big fan of using the expression 'heads-up'. It means to give someone an advance warning. One suggestion of how it came about was from baseball games when the ball was hurtling towards the spectators. If you'd lost interest in the game (and maybe had your head down) the cry of 'heads-up' would have alerted you to danger so you could dodge the oncoming ball.

The Old Testament part of the Bible (that's the bit before Jesus came on the scene) is brimming over with 'heads-ups' about Jesus. In fact someone has worked out that there are well over 300 of them in total. The Bible calls them prophecies and they were advance warnings advertising to the Jewish nation (Israel) that Jesus was on His way to visit earth. Why did God make sure Israel knew that His one and only Son was on the way? Simple. When Jesus eventually rocked up, God wanted to be sure that nobody was in any doubt that Jesus was the special person He'd sent to get us back to being His friends.

In case you wanted to know (and even if you didn't) they called this special person the Messiah. The guys that God used to announce this good news were called prophets and their job

was to keep their ears tuned in to God and then report back to the rest of Israel what He was saying. Sad to say, even though Israel's religious leaders joined in the waiting game for the Messiah, when He finally arrived they rejected Him.

Over the next few pages we're going to take a look at some of these adverts about Jesus and also find out if they were true. Here's one to get you started. In Bible book Micah, chapter 5 and verse 2 it talks about this special person being born in Bethlehem.

See if it was fulfilled in Bible book Matthew, chapter 2 and verse 1.

O n the previous page we found out that the Bible had given a heads-up of where Jesus would be born centuries before it happened. Another heads-up (or prophecy) was all about Jesus' mum-to-be.

It actually came about because a guy called King Ahaz was testing God's patience by refusing to ask Him for proof that He'd keep His promise on a certain matter. God went ahead anyway and gave Ahaz proof positive that His promises would be kept, no matter what. And the way that God decided to prove this was with these words from Bible book Isaiah, chapter 7 and verse 14. Here's how it goes: 'a young woman who is pregnant will have a son and will name him "Immanuel".'

The downside to this heads-up (as far as King Ahaz was concerned) was that it wasn't fulfilled until about 700 years later. So although the king would have been long gone by then (sorry about that, Ahaz) we can take a peek in our Bibles and find out that God was as good as His word (which of course He always is).

In Bible book Matthew, chapter 1 and verses 18 to 23 we can read how things panned out. 'This was how the birth of Jesus Christ took place. His mother Mary was engaged to Joseph, but before they were married, she found out that she was going to have a baby by the Holy Spirit. Joseph was a man who always did what was right, but he did not want to disgrace Mary publicly; so he made plans to break the engagement privately. While he was thinking about this, an angel of the Lord appeared to him in a dream and said, "Joseph, descendant of David, do not be afraid to take Mary to be your wife. For it is by the Holy Spirit that she has conceived. She will have a son, and you will name him Jesus – because he will save his people from their sins." Now all this happened in order to make what the Lord had said through the prophet come true, "A virgin will become pregnant and have a son, and he will be called Immanuel" (which means, "God is with us").'

42
HEADS-UP NO.3

Sad to say not everything to do with the birth of Jesus was happy. Jesus' mum and dad (Mary and Joseph) were obviously over the moon that their first child had been born safe and well. Those well-known shepherds who appear in the Christmas story were thrilled to see for themselves this special baby that an angel had told them about. And the wise men who'd travelled a long, long, way to pay their respects to this new-born King of the Jews were humbled to have had a part to play.

But Herod, the ruler of Israel (where Jesus was born) was not in the mood for hearing these wise men tell him that the star which had led them there signified a new king had been born. As far as King Herod was concerned there was only room for one king in Israel ... and that was him. He certainly wasn't in the mood for giving up his throne any time soon.

King Herod wasn't taking any chances and quickly hatched a dastardly plot to kill Jesus before He got anywhere near his palace. What Herod didn't realise was that Jesus wasn't going to be the sort of king who ruled from a royal residence like his, but a king who would one day rule and reign in heaven. Horrid Herod ordered that every boy under the age of two be

killed in and around Bethlehem (where Jesus had been born) just to make sure that Jesus was eliminated.

There was a heads-up about this in Bible book Jeremiah, chapter 31 and verse 15 which you can check out. For your information, it doesn't actually mention Bethlehem but Ramah which is part of the whole area Herod targeted. You'll be pleased to know that Jesus escaped, but how?

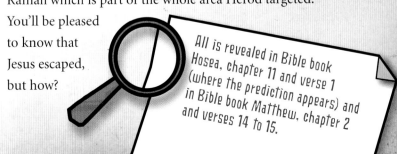

All is revealed in Bible book Hosea, chapter 11 and verse 1 (where the prediction appears) and in Bible book Matthew, chapter 2 and verses 14 to 15.

HEADS-UP NO.4

Although there were some interesting prophecies in the Old Testament part of the Bible (which gave a heads-up to some of the stuff that would be happening during Jesus' life) we're now going to fast-forward to the end of His time on earth. This was the climax of what Jesus had come from heaven to do and God wanted to make sure nobody missed the significance of what was about to take place.

Jesus' plan all along was to allow Himself to be killed as a way of taking the punishment for all the bad stuff us humans do. None of the things that happened to Jesus at the time of His death were by accident, but the people involved didn't know that. First up, Jesus knew that He was going to be betrayed by one of His best buddies, a guy called Judas. Bible book Psalms, chapter 41 and verse 9 predicts this. 'Even my best friend, the one I trusted most, the one who shared my food, has turned against me.' And then in Zechariah, chapter 11 and verse 12 it tells us what Jesus' betrayer got paid for his dirty deed. 'I said to them, "If you are willing, give me my wages. But if not, keep them." So they paid me 30 pieces of silver as my wages.'

Did this all happen as the Bible said? I'm going to let you do some of the leg work for a change. Check out the best buddy

betrayal bit in Bible book Matthew, chapter 26 and verses 20 to 25 and check out the dirty deed dosh bit in Bible book Matthew, chapter 26 and verses 14 and 15. Interesting stuff, eh? In Bible book Zechariah, chapter 11 and verse 13 it also gave a heads-up to what would become of Judas' ill-gotten gains.

To find out what became of Judas you'll need to get back to the Bible again.

The end to this sorry tale is found in Bible book Matthew, chapter 27 and verses 3 to 5.

Thanks to his friend, Judas doing the dirty on Him, Jesus had been arrested by the Jewish religious leaders in a night-time raid. They'd been waiting ages for the chance to nab God's Son and to put Him on trial for breaking their religious laws.

Unfortunately for them they couldn't seem to pin any actual crime on Jesus. To their frustration Jesus was squeaky clean and guilty of nothing deserving a trial. But that wasn't going to stop them from trying to convict Jesus as a criminal. If Jesus needed to be stitched up using the concocted evidence of lying witnesses then that's what they'd do. The bottom line was that the religious leaders wanted Jesus out of the way as fast as possible and if bringing false accusations against Him would achieve this then they were up for it. End of story!

In Bible book Psalms, chapter 35 and verse 11 there was a heads-up warning that this would happen. Here's what it said. 'Evil people testify against me and accuse me of crimes I know nothing about.' I don't know about you but if someone accused me of something I hadn't done I'd be more than tempted to pipe up and say something in my defence. Did Jesus stand His ground and deny the made up charges? Nope! Even when He was put on trial in front of the Roman governor of the region (Pontius Pilate) Jesus continued to remain tight-lipped.

Once again, no surprises that this was also prophesied. You can check out the heads-up bit of this in Bible book Isaiah, chapter 53 and verse 7 and then see how it was fulfilled in Bible book Matthew, chapter 27 and verses 12 to 14. Jesus had a rough ride from the religious leaders and those who were at His trial. The Bible tells us that they spat in His face, hit Him with their fists and that others slapped Him.

What's quite astounding about these Old Testament predictions about Jesus' life is that Jesus was completely up to speed (which is another way of saying that He was totally aware) that these things were going to happen to Him. When you stop to think about some of the stuff that Jesus had to suffer so He could make it possible for us to be friends with God it's amazing that He went through with it, knowing the pain it would cause Him.

In Bible book Isaiah (which has more than its fair share of heads-ups about Jesus) we are told in chapter 53 and verse 12 that Jesus would die alongside wrongdoers (or transgressors). And sure enough that was precisely how things turned out. Jesus was crucified between two criminals. As Jesus hung on the cross taking the punishment for all of the bad things we have ever done the soldiers guarding Him decided to gamble for His clothes. Even that small detail of Jesus' life was given a heads-up by God in Bible book Psalms, chapter 22 and verse 18.

Jesus was executed just before the Jewish Passover feast began and the religious leaders didn't want the bodies of the crucified men left to die during it. I won't go into all the gory details of how it works but the quickest way to finish

them off was to break their legs. Job done. But when the
soldiers who were instructed to carry this out came to Jesus
they discovered that He was dead already (so they didn't
need to break His bones).

Was there a Bible
heads-up for that
as well?

There sure was and you
can find it in Bible book
Psalms, chapter 34 and
verse 20.

46
HEADS-UP NO.7

The last prophecies about Jesus that we're going to take a look at are all to do with His last days on earth. Much to the delight of the religious leaders, Jesus was dead. And as far as they were concerned it was good riddance! They didn't like Jesus one little bit and were glad to finally see the back of Him. Or so they thought!

First off there was the small matter of what to do with Jesus' body. You'll not be surprised if I tell you that God had even sorted this one out back in the Old Testament part of the Bible. In Isaiah chapter 53 and verse 9 it gives the heads-up that Jesus was going to have a burial befitting a rich person. Fast-forward to Bible book Matthew, chapter 27 and verses 57 through to 60 and we are told that on the night of Jesus' death a rich man (called Joseph) rocked up to the Roman governor and asked if he could take Jesus' body and bury it. No probs. Joseph got his wish and Jesus was laid to rest in a tomb that had been intended for Joseph himself.

The story doesn't end there. God had no plans for Jesus to rot in a grave. With Jesus' mission to earth accomplished, God wanted His Son back with Him in heaven. That meant resurrecting Jesus back to life with a new body that was good for earth and that was equally good for heaven. In Bible book Psalms, chapter 16 and verse 10 it gives the heads-up that this was exactly what was going to happen. In fact the Bible says that hundreds of people saw Jesus alive and kicking after His resurrection, including all of His disciples. Wow! Even Jesus' exit from this world was predicted by God. The prophecy about it shows up in Bible book Psalm, chapter 110 verse 1.

47 GOD'S TOP TEN

Everywhere you look there seem to be lists of the top ten this or the top ten that. It's one way of finding out what's popular and what matters most to us. Sometimes it's for fun and other times it's a lot more serious. The Bible has a 'top ten' list that is definitely not just for fun and which God most certainly intended people to take seriously.

If you haven't guessed already, I'm talking about the Ten Commandments. Let me tell you about them. The Israelites had been chosen by God to be His special nation. Their job was to show all the other nations what God was like. It wasn't that easy and, try as they might, the Israelites kept making a hash of things. What the Israelites really needed were some helpful guidelines to show them the things they *should* be doing and the things they *shouldn't*. With a few handy rules in place, doing things God's way ought to be a breeze. So God invited Moses (the leader of the Israelites) up to the top of a mountain to give him these Ten Commandments.

There were no iPads or Post-It Notes® for God to jot them down on in those days, so God settled for two stone slabs and had these rules carved onto them. Did these top ten 'dos and don'ts' make living God's way easy peasy? Nope! But God had known

that all along. First off, God simply wanted the Israelites to know what mattered to Him the most. God's long term plan was that one day people would have such a good relationship with Him, they'd live according to these rules without even trying.

For now though it would have to be a case of them *choosing* to live God's way.

To discover what was top of God's top ten take a look in Bible book Exodus, chapter 20 and verses 1 to 3.

48

WACKY WORSHIP

We're having a sneaky peek at the Ten Commandments to see how God expected the Israelites to live.

Number two on God's list was to do with worshipping idols. So what's that all about then? Although the Israelites worshipped God, not everyone did. To be fair, not everyone had heard about the God of Israel, so it was the Israelites' job to tell people.

It's a fact that most people look for something to worship or to give the No.1 place in their lives. Some people worship pop stars as if they are the most important thing in the world and other people drool over money as if nothing else matters. The Bible calls all those things idols. But in the Old Testament times (and in some places round the world even today) people bowed down to objects or images made from wood, gold or stone that represented the god they worshipped. These are the sort of idols that the Israelites would have known that God was meaning. Why was God so hot on this? I'll tell you.

The Israelites had been slaves in Egypt for hundreds of years and had seen first-hand all the different gods that the Egyptians worshipped. It was now time to forget all that and to concentrate on the one true God who had rescued them.

Because the nations surrounding the Israelites were big on worshipping idols, this was one command that would keep them on the straight and narrow (if they obeyed it). God also added a couple of other rules to help the Israelites keep focused on Him. One of them was to be sure to respect God's name and not to use it as a swear word. God also set aside one day a week for this special nation to take a break and to spend some extra time with Him. As a bit of an encouragement to keep His commands God had an added incentive up His sleeve.

49

SIX OF THE BEST

So far we've checked out four of God's Ten Commandments that were given to the Israelites and now it's time for number five. The first four were all to do with putting God first in our lives but I wonder what sort of thing would be next on God's list?

For God, the next most important thing was to do with our parents. The Israelites were told that showing your parents respect was an absolute must. Why do you think this mattered to God? Well, for one reason, if we treat our parents well and don't keep bad-mouthing them, then respecting others will come far more naturally to us. As an added incentive to keep this rather important command God threw in the promise of a long life for obeying it. Sounds like a good deal to me.

Now for the final five commandments. These were all to do with how we treat other people and how they should treat us. 'Do not commit murder' is number six and makes perfect sense. All people are special in God's eyes and killing another person is a big no-no as far as God is concerned. Next up, God had something to say to husbands and wives. 'Do not commit adultery.' God knows that it hurts married couples when they stop loving each other and this command was His way of trying to protect them. If command number eight was obeyed then the police would have a lot more time on their hands. 'Do not steal' was how God put it. Nearly there. We're now up to number nine and it's the command not to lie about someone else. God always tells the truth and so should we.

Right, we're just about done. Command number ten is all about why people often steal things (and break command number eight).

50

HAPPY ENDING

When it comes to writing a book, the advice that's often given is to make sure it has a beginning, a middle and an end. Although the Bible is not a story book, it still fits the bill when it comes to this handy writing tip.

The Bible begins with giving us the lowdown on how the world came into being at the very beginning of time. It then tells the story of how the people God had created turned their backs on Him and how things went from bad to worse as a result. So that's the beginning bit. But the story didn't end there.

The Bible goes on to tell how God set about getting us back to being His friends. This is the middle bit. How did God do this? Well, in a nutshell, God launched a brand new nation (Israel) so that He could remind people that He was still alive and kicking. God then sent Jesus to be born in Israel and to take the punishment for people turning their backs on God. With His mission accomplished, Jesus went back to heaven, but not before He'd trained up a team of people to tell the world that God had forgiven them.

The very last book of the Bible goes by the name of Revelation. This is where we get to read about how it all ends.

God's plan was not only to make it possible for us to be friends with Him again but also for us to live in a wonderful, unspoiled world once more. That would mean the whole universe getting a make-over from God.

Is that possible? It sure is! Time to read about the Bible's happy ending.

Off you go to Bible book Revelation, chapter 21 and verses 1 to 4.

NATIONAL DISTRIBUTORS

UK: (and countries not listed below)
CWR, Waverley Abbey House, Waverley Lane, Farnham, Surrey GU9 8EP.
Tel: (01252) 784700 Outside UK (44) 1252 784700 Email: mail@cwr.org.uk

AUSTRALIA: KI Entertainment, Unit 21 317-321 Woodpark Road, Smithfield,
New South Wales 2164. Tel: 1 800 850 777 Fax: 02 9604 3699
Email: sales@kientertainment.com.au

CANADA: David C Cook Distribution Canada, PO Box 98, 55 Woodslee Avenue,
Paris, Ontario N3L 3E5. Tel: 1800 263 2664 Email: sandi.swanson@davidccook.ca

GHANA: Challenge Enterprises of Ghana, PO Box 5723, Accra.
Tel: (021) 222437/223249 Fax: (021) 226227 Email: ceg@africaonline.com.gh

HONG KONG: Cross Communications Ltd, 1/F, 562A Nathan Road, Kowloon.
Tel: 2780 1188 Fax: 2770 6229 Email: cross@crosshk.com

INDIA: Crystal Communications, 10-3-18/4/1, East Marredpalli, Secunderabad –
500026, Andhra Pradesh. Tel/Fax: (040) 27737145
Email: crystal_edwj@rediffmail.com

KENYA: Keswick Books and Gifts Ltd, PO Box 10242-00400, Nairobi.
Tel: (020) 2226047/312639 Email: sales.keswick@africaonline.co.ke

MALAYSIA: Canaanland, No. 25 Jalan PJU 1A/41B, NZX Commercial Centre,
Ara Jaya, 47301 Petaling Jaya, Selangor. Tel: (03) 7885 0540/1/2 Fax: (03) 7885 0545
Email: info@canaanland.com.my

Salvation Publishing & Distribution Sdn Bhd, 23 Jalan SS 2/64, 47300 Petaling Jaya,
Selangor. Tel: (03) 78766411/78766797 Fax: (03) 78757066/78756360
Email: info@salvationbookcentre.com

NEW ZEALAND: KI Entertainment, Unit 21 317-321 Woodpark Road, Smithfield,
New South Wales 2164, Australia. Tel: 0 800 850 777 Fax: +612 9604 3699
Email: sales@kientertainment.com.au

NIGERIA: FBFM, Helen Baugh House, 96 St Finbarr's College Road, Akoka, Lagos.
Tel: (01) 7747429/4700218/825775/827264 Email: fbfm_1@yahoo.com

PHILIPPINES: OMF Literature Inc, 776 Boni Avenue, Mandaluyong City.
Tel: (02) 531 2183 Fax: (02) 531 1960 Email: gloadlaon@omflit.com

SINGAPORE: Alby Commercial Enterprises Pte Ltd, 95 Kallang Avenue #04-00,
AIS Industrial Building, 339420. Tel: (65) 629 27238 Fax: (65) 629 27235
Email: marketing@alby.com.sg

SRI LANKA: Christombu Publications (Pvt) Ltd, Bartleet House, 65 Braybrooke
Place, Colombo 2. Tel: (9411) 2421073/2447665 Email: dhanad@bartleet.com

USA: David C Cook Distribution Canada, PO Box 98, 55 Woodslee Avenue, Paris,
Ontario N3L 3E5, Canada. Tel: 1800 263 2664 Email: sandi.swanson@davidccook.ca

CWR is a Registered Charity – Number 294387
CWR is a Limited Company registered in England – Registration Number 1990308

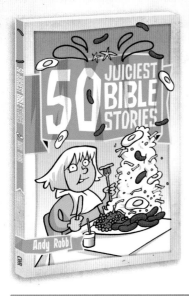

50 Juiciest Bible Stories

Learn about some unusual Old Testament characters and their dastardly deeds before exploring the guidelines that Jesus gave us for living peaceful, happy lives that honour God. Andy Robb, author of the Professor Bumblebrain series, has collected together the juiciest passages of Scripture in *50 Juiciest Bible Stories*. Andy's witty and conversational style plus colourful illustrations brings God's Word to life.

ISBN: 978-1-85345-984-9

50 Jammiest Bible Stories
ISBN:
978-1-85345-851-4

50 Weirdest Bible Stories
ISBN:
978-1-85345-489-9

50 Barmiest Bible Stories
ISBN:
978-1-85345-852-1

50 Wildest Bible Stories
ISBN:
978-1-85345-529-2

50 Goriest Bible Stories
ISBN:
978-1-85345-530-8

50 Craziest Bible Stories
ISBN:
978-1-85345-490-5

For current prices visit www.cwr.org.uk

MORE FROM ANDY ROBB

Professor Bumblebrain offers some exciting explanations, colourful cartoons and (ahem) 'hilarious' jokes answering these important questions:

Who is God? What is He like? Where does He live? How can I get to know Him?
ISBN: 978-1-85345-579-7

Who's the bravest? Who's the funniest? Who's the jammiest? Who's the strongest?
ISBN: 978-1-85345-578-0

Who is Jesus? Where did He come from? What was His mission? What's it to me?
ISBN: 978-1-85345-623-7

Who made the universe? How old is planet earth? What about dinosaurs? Was there really a worldwide flood?
ISBN: 978-1-85345-622-0

Learn about the meaning behind The Prodigal Son, The Wise and Foolish Man, The Lost Sheep and many more!
ISBN: 978-1-85345-947-4

What is prayer? How can we use it? Does it work? Who in the Bible used it?
ISBN: 978-1-85345-948-1

Get into God's Word

Topz is a popular bimonthly devotional for 7- to 11-year-olds.

The Topz Gang teach you biblical truths through daily Bible readings, word games, puzzles, riddles, cartoons, competitions and simple prayers.

Available as an annual subscription (6 bimonthly issues includes p&p) or as single issues (excludes p&p).

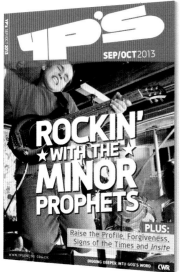

YP's is a dynamic bimonthly devotional for 11- to 15-year-olds.

Each issue is packed with cool graphics, special features and articles, plus daily Bible readings and notes for two months.

Available as an annual subscription (6 bimonthly issues includes p&p) or as single issues (excludes p&p).

For current prices visit **www.cwr.org.uk**
Available online or from Christian bookshops.

Topz SECRET STORIES

from Alexa Tewkesbury

The Topz Secret Stories are full of fun as they help you discover things about yourselves and God. They include humour, relevance and spiritual insight as the rival Dixons gang present problems and opportunities to the Topz gang.

Danny and the Runaway
ISBN: 978-1-85345-991-7

The Cloudgate Mystery
ISBN: 978-1-85345-992-4

One Too Many For Benny
ISBN: 978-1-85345-915-3

Pantomime Pandemonium
ISBN: 978-1-85345-916-0

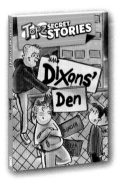

Dixon's Den
ISBN: 978-1-85345-690-9

Dixon's and the Wolf
ISBN: 978-1-85345-691-6

For current prices, visit **www.cwr.org.uk/store**
Available online or from Christian bookshops.